EYE ON SPACE

Space Watch: The Sun

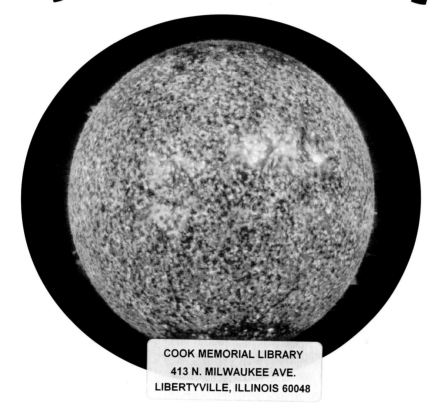

Chris Oxlade

PowerKiDS
press™
New York

Published in 2011 by The Rosen Publishing Group Inc.
29 East 21st Street, New York, NY 10010

First Edition

Editor: Julia Adams
Designer: Robert Walster
Picture researcher: Julia Adams

Library of Congress Cataloging-in-Publication Data

Oxlade, Chris.
  Space watch. The sun / Chris Oxlade. — 1st ed.
     p. cm. — (Eye on space)
  Includes index.
  ISBN 978-1-61532-543-6 (library binding)
  ISBN 978-1-61532-550-4 (paperback)
  ISBN 978-1-61532-551-1 (6-pack)
  1. Sun—Juvenile literature. 2. Solar system—Juvenile literature.
  I. Title. II. Title: Sun.
  QB521.5.O95 2010
  523.7—dc22
                                    2009044619

Photographs:
Alamy: NASA images 10, imagebroker 11, Corbis Super
RF 13, Alex Segre 18, Will Stanton 19, Terrance Klassen
21; iStockphoto: Andreas Weber 20; Science Photo
Library: Detlev van Ravenswaay 4/5, Mehau Kulyk 9,
John Foster 17, SOHO/ESA/NASA 8, Roger Harris 7,
John Bova 16; Shutterstock: Nataliya Peregudova 2, 15,
silver-john 12, emphimy 14; SOHO (ESA & NASA): OFC;
Andy Crawford: 22, 23.

Manufactured in China
CPSIA Compliance Information: Batch #WAS0102PK: For Further Information
contact Rosen Publishing, New York, New York at 1-800-237-9932

Web Sites

Due to the changing nature of Internet
links, PowerKids Press has developed
an online list of Web sites related to
the subject of this book. This site is
updated regularly. Please use this link
to access this list:
http://www.powerkidslinks.com/eos/sun

☀ Contents

The Solar System

Earth is where we live. It is a planet.
It belongs to a group of eight planets.
All these planets get light and heat
from the Sun.

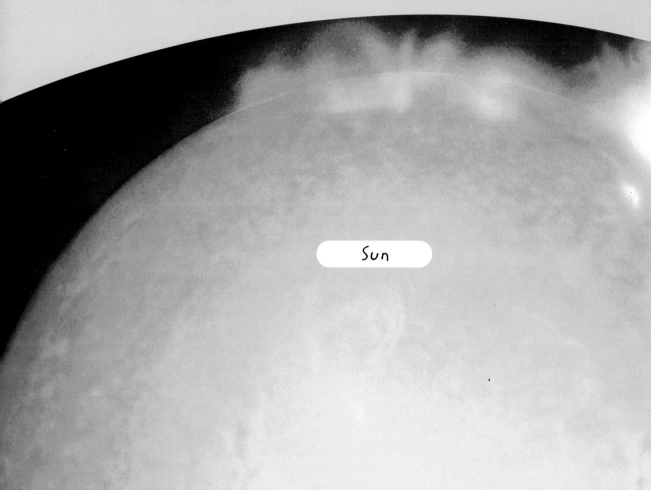

Sun

The eight planets travel around
the Sun in giant circles called orbits.
The Sun and the planets are called
the solar system.

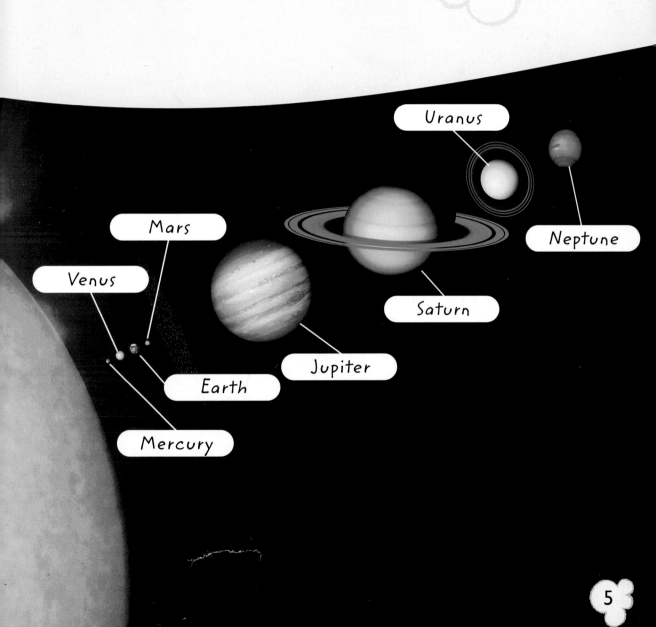

Uranus

Neptune

Mars

Venus

Saturn

Jupiter

Earth

Mercury

 # Sun and Earth

The Sun is a giant ball of glowing gas.
It shines rays of heat and light that travel
through space. They light up all the planets
in the solar system.

The Sun is 70 times wider than the Earth.

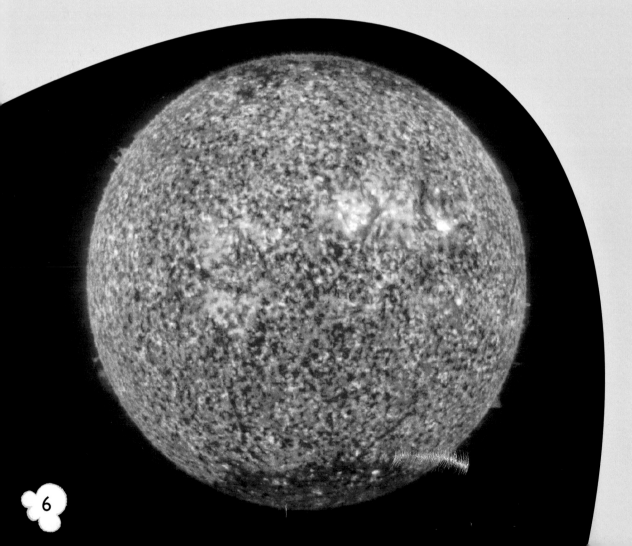

6

The rays of the Sun take more than eight minutes to reach Earth. They are very bright and hot.

From Earth, the Sun looks small because it is very far away.

 # Stars

The Sun is a star. The tiny specks of light in the night sky are stars, too. A star is an object in space that gives off light and heat.

The surface of the Sun is hotter than anything on Earth.

The Sun is a medium-sized star.
Some stars are larger than the
Sun and some are smaller.

You can see many
stars on a clear
night. They are
all farther
away than
the Sun.

Daytime

The Earth spins around once every day.
It is daytime when the place where
you live faces the Sun.

The Sun
only ever
shines on
one side of
the Earth.

Daytime begins when the Sun
rises into the sky.

The Sun rises at a different time each day.

Can you
find out what
time the Sun
rises?

☀ Sunshine

When the Sun shines on our part of the Earth, it gives us light and warmth.

Plants need sunshine to grow.

Sunshine is very bright, so we need
to be careful. Sunscreen protects
our skin from the heat of the Sun.

Without sunscreen, our skin can get burned.

 # Nighttime

It is nighttime when the place where you live faces away from the Sun. Then it is daytime on the other side of the Earth.

daytime

nighttime

At the end of daytime, the Sun goes down in the sky.

Nighttime begins at sunset.

The part of the day when the Sun sets is called dusk.

 Moonlight

On a clear night, you can see the Moon in the sky. The Moon does not make its own light. It is lit up by the Sun.

The Sun only lights up one side of the Moon.

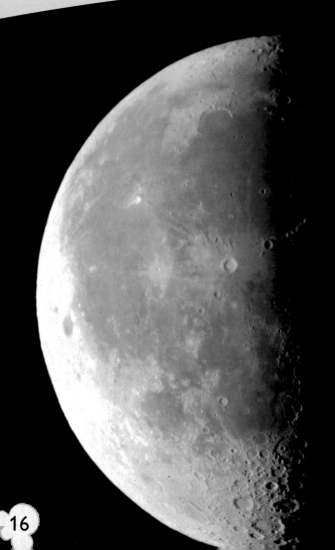

The Moon reflects the light from the Sun to Earth. This is called moonlight.

We only see the part of the Moon that is lit up by the Sun.

☀ The Sun and Life

Without sunshine, the Earth would be a very cold and dark place. There would be no daylight or moonlight.

Heat from the Sun makes the Earth warm.

On other planets in the solar system, it is too hot or cold for things to live.

Without the Sun, we would not have any food to eat. Plants and animals could not live here.

Without sunshine, there would be no fruit or vegetables.

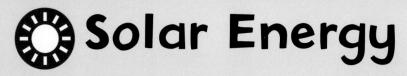 # Solar Energy

The Sun can give us energy. We use energy to make cars move, to work machines, to cook, and to keep warm.

These solar panels use the sunshine to heat water.

We can make electricity from the sunlight. We use solar panels to power some watches, street lamps, calculators, and even cars.

This car is powered by the Sun's energy.

Day and Night

See how sunshine gives us day and night.

You will need:
- a tennis ball (or a ball the same size as a tennis ball)
- a pen • string
- tape
- a flashlight

1. Use a ruler to measure 12 inches (30 cm) of string.

2. Cut the string. Use tape to attach the string to the ball.

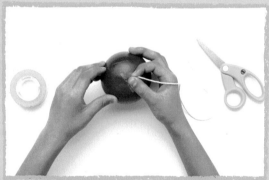

3. With a pen, mark a dot on the ball. This represents where you live.

4. In a darkened room, hold the string so that the ball hangs in the air.

5. Ask a friend to shine a flashlight at the ball from 2 yards away. The flashlight represents the Sun. One side of the ball will be lit up.

6 Spin the ball slowly. Can you see the dot having daytime then nighttime?

Glossary and Further Information

ray light or heat that travels in straight lines

reflects when light bounces off of something

solar panel a panel that collects heat from the Sun or changes sunlight into electricity

star an object in space that gives off light and heat

sunset when the Sun disappears behind the land

Books

Living in Space
by Alex Pang
(Usborne, 2006)

Sun, Moon and Stars
by Kuo Kang Chen
(Usborne, 2006)

The Sun
by Melanie Chrismer
(Children's Press, 2008)

Index